SLAVERY DAYS IN OLD KENTUCKY

SLAVERY DAYS IN OLD KENTUCKY

BY ISAAC JOHNSON, A FORMER SLAVE

A Facsimile of the 1901 Edition
With an Introduction
by
Cornel J. Reinhart

Friends of the Owen D. Young Library and
The St. Lawrence County Historical Association
Canton, New York
1994

DEDICATION

Great-Grandfather,

Although a scurrilous wind blew upon you from a place where your liberties were imprisoned, and your honor defiled, your mind remained a lighted lamp, shining forth great vision, courage, and creative wonders.

My world is better because of you.

Barbara Johnson Felder
June 8, 1993

ACKNOWLEDGEMENTS

I wish to thank a host of local historians and historical associations kind enough to help us follow the trail of Isaac Johnson. Dr. William Hunt, chair, department of history, St. Lawrence University, encouraged this work from the beginning; similarly, Richard Kuhta, University librarian, Owen D. Young Library, St. Lawrence University, graciously lent his coordination skills to the management of the project's entire publication effort. Shirley Tramontana, director of the St. Lawrence County Historical Association, was equally supportive and cooperative, as was E. Jane Layo, Waddington town historian, whose assistance at the Moore Museum in Waddington was simply invaluable. Ms. Hope Marston kindly shared her research on Isaac Johnson's early life and military career. Priceless information and useful leads came from Persis Boyesen, City of Ogdensburg and Town of Oswegatchie historian; Evelyn Watson, Town of Clinton historian; and Lynn Ekfelt, archivist, Owen D. Young Library. Several members of the Baker family were kind enough to talk to us, including Kathleen Baker Goodwin and Kevin and Gary Baker. To my close friend and indefatigable research assistant, Pauline Tedford, deputy Waddington village historian, without whose help this work could not have been done, a heartfelt thanks. A special thanks, as well, to Mrs. Barbara Felder, whose lifelong interest in her great-grandfather's book brought Isaac to life for us all. Lastly, thanks to my wife, Patricia Kelley, for her research insights, interest and considerable patience.

Cornel J. Reinhart

ISAAC JOHNSON
CHRONOLOGY

1844 Isaac Johnson was born in Elizabethtown, Nelson County, Kentucky, son of Richard Yeager and Jane Johnson.

1851 Isaac sold into slavery at age seven by his father, Richard Yeager, to William Mattingly for seven hundred dollars.

1854 Isaac sold to John Mattingly.
Began work on Mattingly's "stock" farm.

1861 Isaac employed by Captain Smith, Company A, Eighth Michigan. Taken to Detroit.

1864 Isaac enlisted in the First Michigan Colored Infantry (102nd United States Colored Regiment) at Detroit on February 3.
He was twenty years old.

1864 Wounded in the left arm and right hand, Isaac lost the middle finger on his right hand in the battle of Honey Hill, South Carolina, November 30.

1865 Discharged from service, July 4.
Returned to Detroit.

1867 Moved to Morrisburg and Winchester, Ontario, Canada. Began work as mason and stonecutter.

1874 Married Theadocia Allen on December 28. Isaac was thirty years old.

1883 At work on the Winchester United Methodist Church, Winchester, Ontario.

1884 Awarded the contracts for the Waddington Town Hall and the Chamberlain Corners Bridge. Moved family to Waddington, New York.

1888 Laid the cornerstone of the Catholic church in Churubusco, New York.

1890 Settled in Ogdensburg, New York.

1897 Fell from a derrick while cutting stone in a stone quarry, Cornwall, Ontario, November 1.

1901 Completed *Slavery Days in Old Kentucky.*

1905 Isaac Johnson died of a heart attack at his home, 21 Main Street, Ogdensburg, New York, December 5. He was sixty-one years old.

INTRODUCTION

"I little dreamed then what I afterwards learned, that my own father had brought all this change to us, that we were sold by his orders and the three thousand three hundred dollars we were sold for went into his pockets less the expenses of the sale. He had sold his own flesh and blood. That is what made American slavery possible. That is the 'Divine institution' we have heard so much about, the cornerstone of the proposed Confederacy."

This brief, but chilling, observation was written in 1901 by Isaac Johnson, then a respected elderly gentleman living quietly in Ogdensburg, New York. Isaac Johnson's life, however, had been full of turmoil and tragedy. It is our good fortune that a few copies of his autobiographical slave narrative have survived to tell us about his early life in Kentucky.

Isaac Johnson's narrative, *Slavery Days in Old Kentucky*, was recently rediscovered in the archives of the Ogdensburg Public Library through the combined efforts of Persis Boyesen, local historian and Ogdensburg librarian, and E. Jane Layo, Waddington town historian. The narrative was, in fact, never lost but had simply not received the kind of attention, or wide distribution, accorded most slave narratives. Privately printed in 1904 in Ogdensburg, the document did find its way to the library of Eastern Kentucky University, to the Owen D. Young library archives at St. Lawrence

University, and to the special collections of the Ogdensburg Public Library. Conversations with the W.E.B. DuBois Center at Harvard University led to a search of the DuBois Center's extensive bibliographic data base, yielding the information that neither Isaac Johnson nor his narrative were recorded. Further discussions with persons at the Schomberg Collection of the New York Public Library produced the same negative result. Essentially, Isaac Johnson and his remarkable slave narrative did not exist, at least for scholars and the general public.

To be precise, *Slavery Days in Old Kentucky* is not a "classic" slave narrative.[1] It was not produced as an anti-slavery document; it was written nearly a half-century after the end of the Civil War and the demise of the "peculiar institution." Still, from the bitter, ironic reference to the "Divine institution," Isaac indicates that he is aware of the growing national rapprochement of North and South, a reconciliation sealed by legalizing segregation and romanticizing the Old South of slavery, plantations and "faithful old darkies." It is a reconciliation and a rendering of the past that he is unwilling to accept.

Isaac's harrowing account of his own young life during those "old slavery days" dispels any possible notion that slavery might have had at least some benign aspect. Isaac's unflinching narrative strikes at the secret heart of the institution. Isaac's father, Richard Yeager, was a white man of Irish descent, who lived for the first seven years of Isaac's life with his Madagascar "wife" and their children in the same small home. There were no slave quarters. This was not the grand plantation of "ole massa" and faithful retainers. This was, by Isaac's account—an account verified in every other particular by the documentary record—a happy, if modest home;

a man and wife with their children. It was also, as it turned out, the dwelling of a slavemaster and his slaves. The slavemaster prevailed; Isaac, his three brothers Louis, Ambrose and Eddie, and his mother, Jane, were each placed on the auctioneer's block and sold into slavery, utterly betrayed and deserted by their father for the price of their sale.[2]

But it is not Richard Yeager, not his father, that Isaac condemns so much as he does the "Divine institution we have heard so much about." Isaac wants a new generation of Americans— indeed, he wants "the world"—to know the truth about slavery. His deeply moving story tells that truth. It does so with as much force today as it did when he first wrote nearly a century ago.

Isaac's youthful experience, however, also required his choosing: in the same breath used to denounce slavery, Isaac emphatically affirms his own skin color, his own blackness; he is horrified by the thought of any association with "a man who could sell his own children or who would uphold a system that enabled him to do so." In words that evoke those of W.E.B. DuBois, Isaac proudly concludes: "My people, for I call only the colored people mine, suffered for centuries, and the only wonder to me is that so many have survived, that they are as intelligent as they are, and as forgiving as they have shown themselves to be."

There is more, of course: the torture and murder of his friend Bob, the wrenching reality of "stock farming," the details of his escape and return. These are the aspects of his life that Isaac thought important enough to want to share with his turn-of-the-century audience. Those of us who read *Slavery Days* for the first time, however, want to know more about Isaac Johnson, about the entire life and career of a man who lived a half-century beyond the end of slavery, and more about a man who could write such an eloquent account of his youth.

What happened to this proud young black man? Where did he go after leaving Kentucky? How did he earn a living? How did he come to live and write his narrative in Ogdensburg, New York, on the St. Lawrence River in the northernmost region of New York State? We are interested for other reasons. Can his life tell us anything about his character or the character of the late nineteenth century? As we contemplate what his later life held, may we hope that his untold story will provide inspiration for us all, of every gender and color, as this nation prepares to enter another century troubled still by the same concerns that confronted a newly free Isaac Johnson?

Almost in passing, Isaac mentions that he enlisted at Detroit, Michigan, in Company A of the newly organized 102nd United States Colored Regiment. He did so to "fight for myself and my race. . ." The date was February 3, 1864. Isaac was twenty years old.

As early as 1861, the leaders of the black community in Detroit met at the Second Baptist Church, where they declared they would sacrifice "to the last extremity" in support of the Union cause.[3] The 102nd United States Colored Regiment organized initially as the First Michigan Colored Infantry, but not without considerable opposition from some members of white society, led by virulent editorials in the Detroit *Free Press*. The principal voice of the Democratic Party in Michigan, the *Free Press* derided the idea of black troops, insisting the only value of raising a black regiment would be to rid Detroit of its black population.

Disregarding these attacks, the First Michigan Colored Infantry was raised by Colonel Henry Barns, the abolitionist editor of the Republican Detroit *Daily Ad-*

vertiser and Tribune. In March 1864 the new regiment took the field under the command of Colonel H.L. Chipman, a captain in the regular army. The organization of the First Michigan Colored Infantry followed by a year the recruitment of the first black troops to serve in the 54th Massachusetts Infantry, immortalized in the moving film *Glory* and led by their white abolitionist officer, Colonel Robert Gould Shaw.

Private Johnson left Michigan on March 28, 1864, for Annapolis, Maryland, where his unit, the First Michigan Colored Infantry, joined the federal Ninth corps, becoming the 102nd United States Colored Regiment. Quickly dispatched, transports carried the 102nd to Hilton Head, South Carolina, arriving on the 16th of April.[4] Isaac and his fellow troopers performed fatigue and picket duty on Hilton Head and St. Helena islands most of the summer and did much the same after federal troops occupied Port Royal. Sent to Jacksonville, Florida, the regiment came under fire for the first time when attacked by Confederate cavalry, easily repulsing the Confederates. The brief engagement brought relief and apparent satisfaction to both officers and men for their conduct under fire.

Following a long and tedious march through eastern Florida, the 102nd returned to Beaufort, South Carolina, in September. Soon these still largely untested black troops met the enemy in several major battles.[5] Charged with destroying the Charleston and Savannah Railroad, Isaac's troop fought side by side with white and black regiments that included the 25th Ohio, the 56th and 155th New York, the 26th, 32nd, 35th and 102nd U. S. Colored, and the 54th and 55th Massachusetts Colored. Beginning in late November 1864, the 102nd Colored engaged the confederates in a series of sharp encounters that continued through April 1865.

On the 30th of November, 1864, at a place called Honey Hill, South Carolina, the 102nd was bloodied.

John Robertson's standard history *Michigan During the War* characterizes the detachment of the 102nd that fought at Honey Hill, or Grahamsville, as receiving the highest commendation of the officers in command for the determination the regiment displayed in holding its ground under severe fire.[6] The expedition's artillery suffered severely from the enemy's fire; so many horses were killed that two guns had to be temporarily abandoned, soon after hauled off the field by the 102nd and saved. Many of the men, though wounded and bleeding, refused to go to the rear and fought until the battle was concluded.

Isaac was seriously wounded in the right hand, losing his middle finger. He was also shot three separate times in the left arm. The three bullets were never removed, causing Isaac some disability in that arm for the remainder of his life.[7] Taken to the rear, Isaac was treated for these serious wounds at the federal hospital in Beaufort, South Carolina. Sixty-six Union officers and men were killed at Honey Hill, 645 others wounded.

After a brief respite, Isaac returned to his regiment perhaps in time to be present at the battle of Deveaux's Neck, South Carolina, on December 9, 1864. The 102nd again joined numerous federal units including the 56th and 155th New York, the 25th and 107th Ohio, the 26th, 33rd and 34th U. S. Colored, the 54th and 55th Massachusetts Colored, the Third Rhode Island Artillery and federal gunboats. The combined Union forces lost 39 killed and 390 wounded; 200 were listed as missing. The Confederate forces suffered nearly 400 dead and wounded.[8]

April 1865 saw the last significant combat of the war for the black troops of the 102nd. Isaac was again wounded, this time hit by a shell fragment that struck his heel on April 9. While not as serious, this injury hampered Isaac through the last months of the war, finally requiring treatment in early August. The 102nd spent the summer of 1865 engaged in guard duty and fatigue operations in several locations around Charleston.

On September 30, 1865, the 102nd United States Colored Troops were mustered out of federal service, proudly returning to Detroit as the battle-tested veterans of the First Michigan Colored Infantry. Ironically, their greatest tribute, perhaps, appeared in the Detroit *Free Press*, acknowledging that the black regiment "fought nobly."[9]

Twenty-one years old, five feet, eight inches tall, light complected (described as yellow-skinned in this era) with black eyes and hair, Isaac Johnson had, in the most literal of meanings, freed himself. Still, his immediate concern was to return to his former plantation in Kentucky to see his old master and to learn what he could of his own people. It was not an especially happy visit. Nevertheless, Isaac spent nearly two years in Kentucky before finally deciding to return to Detroit, where he crossed at Windsor, Ontario, into Canada, the Canaan of his dreams during slavery and a place he was never to travel far from again.

Briefly employed as a sailor on the Great Lakes, Isaac's voyages brought him to the St. Lawrence River port of Morrisburg, Ontario, shortly after he returned from visiting Kentucky. Isaac spent the next decade in and around the small villages in Upper Canada that depended on the St. Lawrence River for so much of their economic and social life in these years. Connecting Upper Canada to Waddington, New York, by means of ferries and numerous other river craft, the St. Lawrence had a long history as one of the most important water highways in North America.

Isaac rather quickly turned his hand to the career that occupied his attentions for the remainder of his life. Finding his way directly north of Morrisburg to the bucolic farming community of Winchester, Isaac began the work for which he is still well remembered in local lore. He must have made quite an impression in this quiet, almost entirely white, Scottish and Irish community; a confident and handsome black man, sporting thick, wide sideburns reaching nearly to the tip of his strong jaw, a former slave, with wounds, indeed, with bullets still in his arm from his service during the American Civil War, Isaac Johnson must have attracted considerable comment and attention.

Isaac drifted north, settling in Winchester around 1870. We know little more about him at this time than his service records provide. As a slave in Kentucky he considered himself a farmer; he served with distinction in the Civil War and worked as a sailor for a short while after the war. In Winchester we can begin to trace his movements, marking his career, by encountering directly the significant stone structures erected by Isaac Johnson, contractor and master mason. Taken together, Isaac's works of stone comprise the monumental legacy of one person, a former Kentucky slave, a black man in a white culture, that remains today as a significant, if almost forgotten, individual contribution to the public culture of Upper Canada and northern New York.

We do not know where or how Isaac acquired his skill as a mason or his experience and talent as an entrepreneurial contractor. We are reasonably certain of this much. Isaac moved around the Winchester region for a short time, eventually settling into a log home across the road from the Baker quarry on the farm owned and operated by the Baker family today. In what was a truly electrifying moment Pauline Tedford and I encountered persons for whom Isaac Johnson was more than a dim historical figure. Isaac is remembered still, by the present Baker generation, as the man respectfully referred to by their father, Earl Baker, now deceased, as Mr. Johnson. In stories told to them during their childhood years, Mr. Johnson is credited with developing the potential of the limestone quarry and, in fact, with building the impressive stone house occupied by members of the Baker family to this day.

Historians typically pursue their searches through libraries and great piles of dusty archival paper. The almost casual announcement, quickly followed by the dramatic presentation, of an outdated sledgehammer, worn and rusty, accompanied by a matching solid iron prybar six feet in length, whose sole purpose was to separate layered stone, brought me, for a brief instant, face to face with the living Isaac Johnson.

Isaac worked on several other private stone homes in the immediate region, employing a crew of men as stonecutters in the winter and masonry laborers during the milder seasons. It seems reasonable to believe that he also worked on other public buildings in nearby villages during these same years.

While living in Winchester, around 1873, Isaac found time to build and carve a chair for a young friend, Katherine Scott. The smallest but in some ways the most revealing and interesting of Isaac's surviving artifacts, this chair resides today in the Moore Museum in Waddington, New York. It is strikingly different from the other English and American furniture pieces displayed in the museum. Coal black, Isaac's chair is utterly distinctive with its carved African patterns and markings. At first glance, the museum visitor knows the carver drew on non-western resources for inspiration. There is no better, or more vivid, expression of Isaac Johnson's African heritage.

Now thirty years old, having established his reputation as a stonecutter and mason, Isaac Johnson married Theadocia Allen in Morrisburg, Ontario, on December 28th, 1874. We know precious little about Theadocia. She was born in New York State of Canadian parents, John and Louise Allen.[10] The single extant photograph of Theadocia, published in Isaac's narrative, suggests a person of considerable pride and determination; her piercing confident gaze is unflinching, and we suspect she was much the same.

Theadocia gave birth to their first child, a daughter, Gertrude, in Winchester on October 4, 1876. Gertrude was nearly five before her sister Susan was born in June 1881, also in Ontario.

Isaac's reputation as a stone mason seems to have kept pace with his growing family responsibilities. In early 1881 the Episcopal Methodists of Winchester began actively contemplating the erection of a new United Methodist Church. John Benjamin Baker, church trustee and owner of the Baker quarry, served on the building committee. Strongly favoring the project, Mr. Baker agreed to supply the project's required stone and lime for one thousand dollars. For that amount, John Benjamin Baker, commonly called Ben, and his six sons labored on the project for an entire year. Near the end of this period Ben Baker was seriously injured lifting a large stone window sill from a wagon at the construction site. Mr. Baker suffered a rupture of his stomach lining from which he never recovered. He died in 1884, leaving the church unfinished.

Undoubtedly the injury and subsequent death of Mr. Baker, the project leader, necessitated new construction arrangements. The official history of the Winches-

ter United Church does not make clear how Isaac
Johnson came to direct the final work, but his contribution is vividly recalled: "A legend has arisen about his
work. It is said that the north wall had been raised to
the tops of the windows when he found it out of line by
half an inch." *A History of Winchester United Church,
1883-1983* continues, "satisfied with nothing less than
perfection, he tore it down to begin again."[11]

Erected in the heart of Winchester, the completed
United Church provided a magnificent centerpiece for
the village. A dignified gray stone structure, the church
is flanked on its northwestern face by an imposing
stone bell tower. The handsomely proportioned sanctu-
ary, like the bell tower, was graced with a traditional
slate roof when finally completed in 1886.

Even before the roof was finished, Isaac accepted two
new and important public contracts from the Town of
Waddington, New York. Situated directly opposite
Morrisburg, Ontario, on the St. Lawrence River, Waddington was a busy industrial port. Founded shortly
after the beginning of the nineteenth century, by 1884
Waddington had reached the peak of its commercial
and industrial potential. The St. Lawrence provided
both transportation for trade and travel; ferries and
packet boats plied the river, making travel to Morrisburg, Montreal and nearby Ogdensburg easy and inex-
pensive. Dammed and channeled, the St. Lawrence at
Waddington also powered the several industries that
lined the river's bank—the first sight to impress a visitor approaching Waddington aboard a ferry from the
Canadian shore.

On February 12, 1884, at their annual town meeting
the voters of Waddington authorized the expenditure of
eight thousand dollars for the building of a town hall;
at the same meeting the town property owners bud-

geted an additional four thousand dollars to allow construction of a bridge over the Grass River at Chamberlain Corners. Isaac Johnson bid on, and received, the contract to build both of these substantial public structures.

Adopting the techniques he had learned and developed in Upper Canada, Isaac now faced the responsibility of undertaking the construction of two large stone structures simultaneously. Three crews would be required, one to cut and transport stone from a nearby quarry, and one each for the bridge and town hall. The work also necessitated moving his young family from their familiar surroundings in Winchester, Ontario, to new quarters in Waddington.

Both of these quite impressive structures stand today. While the architect for the town hall is unknown, the building itself is rather uncomplicated. Essentially a rectangle, the building's narrow end frames the hall's front face looking out upon the village's main street. Similar to the United Methodist Church, Waddington's town hall is also distinguished by an imposing tower standing at the left front of the hall. Situated above a large and useful basement, the main meeting room is reached by climbing twelve wide front stairs. After entering through two cathedral doors, visitors find themselves in a spacious auditorium with a ceiling rising nearly twenty feet from the floor, complete with a stage spanning nearly the entire rear wall.

Currently undergoing restoration, the town hall has been a source of considerable pride and value to the community for over a century. As meeting place, opera house, town office and home to numerous community functions, it is fair to say that Waddington's town hall, built by a former slave born in the American South, has served this northern New York community well during the past one hundred years.

Close by the proposed bridge location, a large brick home, owned by the Chamberlain family, operated as a stagecoach stop and country inn. The Temperance Tavern, as it was (ironically) known, sat astride this important nineteenth-century juncture for travel east and west between Canton and Malone, serving as well to connect Waddington to points south and east. Constructed of five picturesque stone arches, the Chamberlain Corners bridge withstood the ravages of water and ice until it underwent major renovation work in the early 1930s. At a time when so many historic bridges in New York have been replaced, Isaac Johnson's century-old stone bridge at Chamberlain Corners continues to provide useful service for regional travel and commerce. Local citizens and historians alike still consider the Chamberlain Corners bridge one of the area's finest arched stone bridges.[12]

As work on the Chamberlain Corners bridge and Waddington town hall neared completion, the Presbyterian Church in Waddington was destroyed by fire in 1887. In the bidding process that followed, Isaac submitted three successively lower bids. The last and most detailed submission provides a unique glimpse into Isaac's work and responsibilities at this stage in his career: "I hereby tender for the stone work for building the new stone church as set forth in the specifications and plans made by Geo. E. Wilson, architect, Ogdensburg, as follows: I will build and do all the cutting of stone except Butters caps them. I leave rock face and furnish the lime and sand and furnish all the cut stone, scaffolding for the sum of $3,100." Isaac's bids were lower than all his competitors', but in the end the Presbyterian Building Committee rejected his bid, settling on an arrangement with a member of their own congregation to complete the new church.[13]

Now forty-three years of age, Isaac had lived and worked in Waddington for five years. His family had grown larger with two additional daughters: Alice, born in March of 1883, and Hattie, born in Canada in June 1885. On August 12, 1889, Theadocia gave birth to twins, a son and daughter, Louis and Louisa, in Waddington.

During the same month, August 1889, Isaac was once again hard at work on his latest project, constructing the Catholic church at Churubusco, New York, located at the highest point between Ogdensburg and Rouses Point, New York. Isaac traveled easily to Churubusco on the Ogdensburg and Lake Champlain railroad line that connected these important nineteenth-century transshipment ports on the St. Lawrence River and Lake Champlain, respectively. Isaac laid the cornerstone of the new Churubusco Catholic church in 1888. A picture of Isaac and his crew taken in that first year or the next, 1889, identifies Isaac Johnson, "a Negro stone-mason," with other members of his crew including "Beef" Conway of Waddington and the church's pastor, Father Jeremiah P. Murphy. Isaac stands at the center of a group of twenty workmen, the lower walls of the new St. Philomena Church (today the Immaculate Heart of Mary) in the background.[14]

This was the last major building project undertaken by Isaac Johnson that it has been possible to document. We know, however, that he continued to work as a contractor and mason. Lack of further work in or around Waddington and the failure to secure the Presbyterian Church contract undoubtedly required that he move his family once more, now to the bustling St. Lawrence River port city of Ogdensburg, New York. In 1888 construction of one of New York State's massive regional asylums for the insane was begun in Ogdensburg under the direction of an influential member of the State

Board of Charities, William Pryor Letchworth, with the strong support of Governor Roswell Flower. Located at Point Airy on the shores of the St. Lawrence River, the large number of administrative buildings and inmate "cottages," almost all built of stone or brick, provided unparalleled opportunities for work and contracts to local masons and builders. We can assume that Isaac found work for himself and his men on the asylum grounds. Wherever he found work, by 1890, Isaac, Theadocia and the children were living in one of Ogdensburg's quiet residential neighborhoods, at 126 Ford Avenue.

The records, documents and photographs that have allowed us to follow Isaac's life and career to 126 Ford Avenue unfortunately begin to fail us after taking us this far. It seems possible that when he first filed for a disability pension, on April 9, 1889, based on the wounds to his hand and arm during the Civil War, his arm was increasingly impaired. Isaac was not granted a pension on the strength of this application, yet seemed to manage well enough for several more years. He did move again, however, to the heart of the indus- trial section of Ogdensburg, 21 Main Street, nearer to the city quarry, directly in the middle of the city's noisy, unpleasant complex of water-powered mills. Isaac and Theadocia's last child, Daniel, was born to the couple in Ogdensburg, January 21, 1893.

Monday, the first day of November 1897, Isaac's long and successful masonry career abruptly ended when he fell from a derrick while cutting stone at Cornwall, Ontario. He seriously fractured his right ankle. The federal government now granted his renewed pension application, providing a modest allotment of twelve dol- lars a month for him and his family. Gertrude, the el- dest child, now began living and working outside the house, probably providing as much help as she could; the other children remained at home with their father and mother.[15]

Slavery Days in Old Kentucky was written during this difficult period in Isaac's life. An active life of skilled labor and numerous responsibilities afforded little time for reflection. Now injuries, both old and new, provided the opportunity for Isaac to contemplate his past and future. In both instances his first consideration was for his family. *Slavery Days in Old Kentucky* ends with his address: 21 Main Street, Ogdensburg, New York, printed in the hope that any of his relatives might see "this little pamphlet."

As for the future, each of his children was given a hard- bound copy of his narrative and his living relatives today inform us that *Slavery Days* itself was published, not only to remind a larger audience about the truth of slavery, but also to provide an income for his family—specifically to help his children attend college.

Isaac Johnson, slave, soldier, master mason, author, died on December 5, 1905, at his home in Ogdensburg, New York. He was sixty-one years old. The local newspaper reported that Isaac Johnson, "A well-known colored man," died suddenly at home while seated in his chair. Mr. Johnson, the notice continued, "suffered from heart disease for many months and his health was gradually fading."[16] Isaac was buried in the Johnson family plot in the Ogdensburg cemetery. Theadocia was fifty-one years old at the time of Isaac's death; she lived only three years without her husband, dying on March 6, 1908, as quietly as she lived. Her oldest daughter, Gertrude, became the guardian of her youngest brother, Daniel. In time, Gertrude, Susie, Hattie and Daniel were all buried with their parents.

Isaac's story moves us greatly. His *Slavery Days in Old Kentucky* is obviously very special. It joins the relatively few extraordinary accounts we have from the survivors of slavery in the American South.[17] But Isaac's later life, the life he did not believe sufficiently important to record, is of particular interest to us today. It is not heroic in any common meaning of this term. Isaac was simply a husband, a skilled artisan, a dedicated family man. But as our nation, nearly ninety years after Isaac's death, continues to struggle with precisely the same concerns and issues that Isaac addressed so movingly in his *Slavery Days in Old Kentucky*, we realize those same ninety-odd years have not yet provided this nation with sufficient time to create a truly inclusive culture.

Isaac's life speaks to us all, black and white. It is an ordinary life of struggle and achievement; it is a life set amidst an entirely white culture, yet Isaac remains true to his own blackness, his own sense of self. It is a tribute to Isaac, as well as to the larger culture of northern New York and Upper Canada, that his unique talents found expression in this community's most significant structures, sacred and secular. Isaac's life, his singular talents and public contributions emphasize discrimination's true toll; it impels consideration of creative endeavors forever lost. Isaac Johnson inspires all Americans to strike our shackles, to free our minds.

Cornel J. Reinhart
Canton, New York
January, 1994

NOTE ON SOURCES

Isaac's application for an invalid disability pension filed in St. Lawrence County, New York, October 12, 1889 (and a subsequent application on April 5, 1901) provided the first important clue in our effort to trace Isaac's movements in the years after his military discharge. A little crowded in the space the form allowed, Isaac responded to the question concerning his whereabouts since war's end: "first I was a Sailor on the Lakes part of the time in Canada and part of the time in this Country lived in Winchester Canada 7 or 8 years Morrisburg Canada about 2 years and for the last 5 years I have resided in Waddington N.Y." His occupation is listed simply: "Builder and Contractor." Answers to other questions indicated that he was a slave, that his last owners were William and John Mattingly, and that his disability could be traced to the wounds received at the battle of Honey Hill, South Carolina.

The Genealogical Records of the Church of Jesus Christ of Latter-day Saints for Nelson County, Kentucky, 1844, document the birth of only one Isaac Johnson in that year. The 1850 federal Population Census for Nelson County, Kentucky, records the presence of the Richard Yeager household; the 1860 federal Slave Schedules further confirm that John Mattingly of Nelson County owned thirteen slaves, two of whom were sixteen-year-old black males.

Isaac Johnson's later life and career as a contractor, mason and stonecutter was traced through census records in both the United States and Canada, supplemented by Sanborn insurance maps, local newspapers, and church and village records. Local historical associations were extremely cooperative, including the St. Lawrence County Historical Association, Canton, New York; the Moore Museum, Waddington, New York; the research facilities of Upper Canada Village, Morrisburg, Ontario; the Ogdensburg Public Library, Ogdensburg, New York; and the Owen D. Young Library, St. Lawrence University, Canton, New York.

---

[1] For discussion of the slave narrative, and representative examples of the genre, see Henry Louis Gates, Jr., ed., *The Classic Slave Narratives* (New York: New American Library, 1987), Ara W. Bontemps, ed., *Great Slave Narratives* (Boston: Beacon Press, 1969), John W. Blassingame, ed., *Slave Testimony: Two Centuries of Letters, Speeches, Interviews, and Autobiographies* (Baton Rouge: Louisiana State University Press, 1977) and Gilbert Osofsky, *Puttin' on Ole Massa: The Slave Narratives of Henry Bibb, William Wells Brown and Solomon Northup* (New York: Harper and Row, 1969).
[2] Isaac's account of the "stock farm" and trading activities of John and William Mattingly is noted in J. Winston Coleman, Jr., *Slavery Times in Kentucky* (Chapel Hill: University of North Carolina Press, 1940), 155-56. John Mattingly's trading business is also mentioned in the older classic account by Frederic Bancroft, *Slave Trading in the Old South* (Baltimore 1931), 139-140 and cf. T.D. Clark, "The Slave Trade Between Kentucky and the Cotton Kingdom," *Mississippi Valley Historical Review*, XXI, December 1934, 331-341.

³The most useful source for the history of the First Michigan Colored Infantry (102nd United States Colored Troops) can be found in Michael O. Smith, "Raising A Black Regiment in Michigan: Adversity and Triumph," *Michigan Historical Review*, XVI, 2, 1990, 22-41. Also cf. John Robertson, comp. *Michigan in the War* rev. ed. (Lansing, Michigan: W.S. George and Co., 1882).

⁴Smith, "Raising A Black Regiment in Michigan," 39.

⁵Robertson, *Michigan in the War*, 490-1.

⁶*Ibid*.

⁷Isaac Johnson, *Service Records*, National Archives, Washington, D.C.

⁸Smith, "Raising a Black Regiment In Michigan," 40, and Benson J. Lossing, *Mathew Brady's Illustrated History of the Civil War* (The Fairfax Press, 1912), 448.

⁹Smith, "Raising a Black Regiment In Michigan," 41, Robertson, *Michigan in the War*, 493.

¹⁰From Theadocia's death certificate on file at the Ogdensburg city clerk's office.

¹¹*A History of Winchester United Church, 1883-1983* (The United Church of Canada, Winchester, Ontario), 16.

¹²Pauline Tedford, *Waddington: A Look At Our Past* (Ogdensburg, New York: Ryan Press, 1976) 31-32.

¹³Isaac Johnson to Building Committee, Presbyterian Church, April 1888, *Presbyterian Church Records*, Waddington, New York. Cf. similar letters of January 20 and February 28, 1888.

¹⁴This important photograph was brought to our attention by Evelyn Watson, Town of Clinton historian. The original has been lost but happily it was reproduced in the *North Country Catholic*, May 16, 1967.

¹⁵1900 federal census for Ogdensburg shows Theadocia Johnson as head of household at 21 Main Street in Ogdensburg with five of her children: Alice, Hattie,

Louis, Louisa and Daniel. Gertrude is recorded as a servant in the household of George Malby. Susie is listed as a boarder in Theadocia's household. Isaac was probably living temporarily in Ottawa, Canada, perhaps seeking some compensation for the injury he sustained while working in Cornwall, Ontario.

[16]Ogdensburg *Advance and St. Lawrence Weekly Democrat*, Ogdensburg, New York, December 7, 1905.

[17]In addition to the slave narratives noted above, see the unique selections taken from the Slave Narrative Collection of the Federal Writer's Project by B. A. Botkin, *Lay My Burden Down: A Folk History of Slavery* (Chicago: 1945) and Norman R. Yetman, ed., *Voices from Slavery* (New York: Holt, Rinehart and Winston, 1970).

ISAAC JOHNSON,
THE AUTHOR.

SLAVERY * *
* * * * DAYS
IN OLD KENTUCKY.

BY ISAAC JOHNSON, A FORMER SLAVE.

REPUBLICAN & JOURNAL CO. PRINT,
OGDENSBURG N. Y.

PREFACE.

The present generation knows but little of actual slavery. Attempts are sometimes made to color the Institution to make it appear as though the old days of American slavery were patriarchal days to be desired, to surround the Institution with a glamour as though it possessed great intrinsic merits of value to both races. But we believe that any system of human slavery is always degrading both to the master and the slave. The hardships of my slave life were nothing in comparison with many, and the following pages of my actual experience as a slave are given, not for the purpose of casting reflections upon those who favored the Institution, but to give to the world a knowledge of the subject that no eloquence may ever make the same thing again possible.

THE AUTHOR.

Dated September, 1901.

INDEX.

SLAVERY DAYS IN OLD KENTUCKY.

A TRUE STORY OF A FATHER WHO SOLD HIS WIFE AND FOUR CHILDREN. BY ONE OF THE CHILDREN.

CHAPTER I.

IN THE BEGINNING.

So many people have inquired as to the particulars of my slave life and seemingly listened to the same with interest, that I have concluded to give the story in this form.

I was born in the State of Kentucky in 1844. When I first came to a knowledge of myself I was a child living with my parents on a farm located on the banks of Green river in my native State. The family at that time consisted of my father, Richard Yeager, my mother, Jane, an older brother, Louis, a younger brother, Ambrose, and later on another brother, Eddie. I was next to Louis in age. Here we lived a happy and contented family, and prosperous beyond most of the farmers in that section of the State. For reasons that will appear before the end is reached my sur-name is the maiden name of my mother. As I look back to my boyhood days I can see that my mother was an intelligent woman, considering her station in life, and it is from her, and my paternal uncles in after years, I learned as to my ancestry.

My grandfather was an Irishman, named Griffin Yeager, and his brothers were engaged in the villainous vocation of the Slave Trade. Their business was to steal negroes from Africa or wherever they could get

them and sell them as slaves in the United States. My
mother was stolen by these people from the island of
Madagascar in the year 1840.   She was brought to
America and given to my grandfather who concluded
she would make a good servant.   He gave her the name
of Jane and kept her till he died, which was soon after.

By the terms of grandfather's will, Jane was be-
queathed to his eldest son, Richard, commonly known
as Dick Yeager.   Dick also received by the will other
personal property, and, equipped with cows, sheep, horses
and some farming utensils, he took Jane and moved
onto the farm referred to on Green river.   He used
Jane in all respects as a wife and she, in her innocence,
supposed she was such.   I well remember their little
house.   It was about twenty feet by sixteen with a nine
foot ceiling.   It had only one outside door and two
windows.   The house was divided into two rooms, a
kitchen and bed room.   A fireplace occupied a part of
one end, the foundation being large flat stones on which
cooking was done.   Their furniture was limited as well
as their cooking utensils, but these were sufficient for
their wants, and on the whole it was a happy home.   They
at first had no neighbors nearer than ten miles.   They
worked together in harmony, she taking the lead in the
house and he in the field, where she often assisted him.
The first year they raised such vegetables as they need-
ed but these brought no money.   They then commenced
raising tobacco and hogs.   Their first crop of tobacco
brought them $1600 in cash, but the hogs all died.
They were so encouraged by the tobacco crop that they
devoted all their energy to this product thereafter, and
in time they became the leading tobacco growers. Other
people soon came as neighbors, none of whom owned

MRS. THEADOCIA JOHNSON.

slaves. The new comers disapproved of and freely talked about Yeager and his manner of living with a slave and raising children by her. This talk resulted in social ostracism of the Yeager family, notwithstanding he was more prosperous than any of them. Yeager felt the social cut keenly and concluded to sell out and leave that part of the country. He accordingly advertised his farm and stock for sale. At this time his children were aged as follows: Louis was nine years of age, Isaac (myself) was seven, Ambrose five and Eddie was two. The sale took place. He retained the horses which were taken to the New Orleans market, leaving the family during his absence. Here we remained waiting patiently his return, till about two months thereafter, when the sheriff came and took us all to Bardstown in Nelson county, about two days journey eastward, and here we were placed in the negro pen for the night.

CHAPTER II.

THE AUCTION SALE.

The next morning, to our astonishment, a crowd gathered and took turns examining us. What it all meant we could not imagine till Louis was led out about ten o'clock, placed on the auction block and the auctioneer cried out: "How much do I hear for this nigger?" Allow me to say here, it was only the vulgar and low whites who used the term "nigger," the better classes always spoke of us as negroes or colored folks. The auctioneer continued his cry for bids and Louis was at last sold for eight hundred dollars. By this time we had taken in the situation, and it seemed as though my mother's heart would break. Such despair I hope I may never again witness. We children knew something terrible was being done, but were not old enough to fully understand.

Then the auctioneer called for Isaac and I was led out, the auctioneer saying, "Time is precious gentlemen, I must sell them all before night; how much do I hear for this nigger?" We were instructed beforehand that we must answer all questions put to us by "Yes, sir" and "No, sir." I was asked if I had ever been whipped, or sick, or had had the toothache, and similar questions to all of which I answered. He then cried for bids. The first bid was four hundred dollars. This was gradually raised until I was struck off for seven hundred dollars, and sold to William Madinglay, who came forward and said: "Come along with me, boy, you belong to me." I said to him: "Let me go and see my mother." He answered me crossly: "Come along with me, I will train you without your mother's help." I was taken to one side and chained to a post as though I had been a horse. I remained hitched to this post till late in the afternoon.

The next one sold was Ambrose. I could not see him, but I could hear the auctioneer crying for bids and my little four year old brother was sold for five hundred dollars to William Murphy.

The next to be set up was my mother and our little baby boy Eddie. To the cry for bids no one responded for some time and it looked for awhile that they were to escape being sold. But someone called out: "Put them up separately. "Then the cry was: "How much do I hear for the woman without the baby?" The first bid was eight hundred dollars, and this was gradually raised till she was sold for eleven hundred dollars.

The next sale was of Eddie, my little brother, whom we all loved so much, he was sold for two hundred dollars, to one John Hunter. Thus, in a very short time, our happy family was scattered, without even the privilege of saying "Good by" to each other, and never again to be seen, at least so far as I was concerned.

CHAPTER III.

MY NEW HOME.

Late in the afternoon my new master put me into a wagon and took me over very rough and hilly roads to his home about five miles distant, on a farm located on the bank of Beech Fork river. We reached this home of William Madinglay about ten o'clock at night. His wife, one child, and Peter, a slave, constituted his family, and I made one more.

On reaching the place, Madinglay called loudly: "Peter." This individual soon appeared, saying "Yes, sir, Master." He was then asked:

"Have you put in feed for the horses?"

"Yes, sir, Master."

Turning to me he said: "Come along with me."

We went to the kitchen and there we met his wife at the door when she asked: "What have you there, William."

His answer was: "Oh, I have a little boy here for you."

"Indeed, you have a bright little fellow," she replied.

He then said: "This is one of the Yeager niggers we saw advertised for sale at auction."

"I declare he is not a very dark colored one."

"No, wife, he isn't, you see he is one of those pumpkin seed niggers from the mountains."

"Oh Bill! what makes you talk that way? I think he will make a good servant."

His reply was: "I reckon he will when he gets that black snake around him a couple of times." (He referred to the raw hide whip.)

"William, I hope he will not need that at all, I don't think he is as stupid as Peter."

"Oh well, Margaret, I don't mind if he is stupid, I can train him, there is nothing like the black snake for stupidness."

I had never heard such talk before, and I hung my head and began to cry when she said: Oh Bill, don't scare the boy to death, I think he will be a good boy.

Master then commanded: "Stand up there and straighten up, let your Mistress see what kind of a boy you are, she hasn't half seen you yet."

She brought a lamp from the shelf and carefully looked me over, after which she said: "Oh what a nice little lad, and what a nice suit he has on!"

"Oh yes, wife, up on the mountains they don't know how to work the niggers, but I will teach him how to work. The idea of a nigger with a suit on him like that! Wait till I get a suit on him, I'll show him how to work."

She then asked: "What is your name?"

"Isaac," I answered.

"That's a nice little name. Take off your hat, put it on the chair and sit down in the corner."

I took off my hat and coat and looked for a place to hang them, as I had been accustomed to do in our old home, but found none. I laid them on the little bundle I had with me and walked over to the corner of the fireplace and sat on the floor. Peter came in and Master asked: "Have you got your chores all done?"

"Yes, sir, Master."

"Did you go to the mill today?"

"Yes, sir, Master."

"Did you bring a load of meal home?"

"Yes, sir, Master."

"Is there plenty of wood at the still?"

"Yes, sir, Master."

"Do you know if they are going to grind tomorrow?"

"Yes, sir, Master, dey's going to grind tomorrow."

After Master and his wife had eaten their supper, which consisted of mush and milk, she brought us a pan of the same for our supper, after which Master said: "Peter, this is a little nigger who is to help you in your work, he is green, but you must teach him." Mistress then brought an old quilt, saying: "This is a quilt for your bed tonight, you and Peter can sleep together, he will show you."

Peter also had an old quilt, we laid one down and took the other for a cover, our bed being the floor.

Oh, what a change! The sight of Peter set me nearly crazy. All he wore was a long tow shirt, a cloth cap and no shoes. It did not take him long to turn in as he had nothing to take off. I took off my shoes, socks, pants and coat, and then looked around to see what he had for a pillow, and found he had none, but was curled up like a snake. I sat there for hours thinking of my mother, brothers and father until I was nearly wild with the change that had come, changed from a happy home to be used like a dog, and a pretty mean one at that. I wondered if I should ever see my people again. I little dreamed then what I afterwards learned that my own father had brought all this change to us, that we were sold by his orders and the three thousand three hundred dollars we were sold for went into his pockets less the expenses of the sale.   He had sold his own flesh and blood. That is what American slavery made possible.   That is the "Divine institution" we have heard so much about, the cornerstone of the proposed Confederacy.   Is it any wonder the Southerners were defeated with such an incubus around their necks, dragging them down to a condition lower than their slaves, making them human demons!   Do you wonder that when freedom came to me I preferred the maiden name of my sainted mother to the name of my father?   In my ignorance of the true situation I mourned for him in common with my mother and brothers, and sat through that night bewildered, until tired nature forced me to lie down.   I took my little bundle for a pillow, wrapped the quilt about me, not to sleep but rather to dream and wonder what terrible thing had happened to my dear father, as I then thought of him, to bring this misfortune upon us.   I tried to console myself with the thought that there must be some hereafter when we could all meet again sometime.   The night wore away at last but I had had no rest.   Then I heard the mournful voice of Master calling: "Peter, Peter, are you awake?"

"Yes, sir, Master."

"Make the fire in the kitchen and in here."

"Yes, sir, Master."

"Bring Isaac, the lad, and show him what to do."

"Yes, sir, Master."

"Take him with you to do the chores."

"Yes, sir, Master."

"Peter then told me to bring some water while he split some wood for the Mistress.   I asked where I would get the water.

He said: "Se dat tree down dare?"

I said, "Yes."

He said, "You go to dat tree, when you get dare you see nuther tree uther side dat tree, and when you get dare you'll see little grass uther side dat tree, and uther side dat grass dare is big hole and dat is whare de water is."

I went but failed to find "de big hole," and he upbraided me, saying: "You nice nigger! can't fin dat well when it's bin dare long while, long fore I comed here and you can't fin it!"

He took the pail and showed me the well. After we returned he asked: "Do you tink you can fin dat well now?"

I said, "I thought I could," and he sent me for another pailful while he carried in the wood, after which we were to have something to eat.

We went into the house and Mistress asked: "Peter, have you done all the chores?"

"Yes, mam!" said Peter, and we then sat on the floor, Peter in one corner of the fireplace and I in the other; here we sat until Master and Mistress had finished their breakfast when she brought us our mush and milk once more.

Master then came in and said, "Peter!"

"Yes, sir, Master."

"Have you finished your breakfast?"

"Yes, sir, Master."

"Go and hitch up the mules and bring them ready to put on the grist for the mill." We obeyed and the mules were loaded with three sacks of corn on each except two that carried only two sacks each, these last were to be ridden and the others were to be led.

CHAPTER IV.

AT HOME WITH MISTRESS.

Master and Peter went with the mules and I was left to help Mistress do the washing. I was pleased with this arrangement as I liked her better than the Master. She, wishing to learn my skill as a washer, gave me first the baby's soiled clothes, these I cleaned to her satisfaction; she then gave me Master's clothes which I also washed and then she gave me her own clothes, all of which pleased her. She then asked if I could iron. I told her I would try. The clothes were dried and brought in and I ironed all of them. She was kind to me and complimented my work, saying: "You have done very well, my boy, and now you may sit down and rest."

I sat down, but not to rest. The moment I stopped working a great grief came to me so overpowering I could not conceal my feelings and I began to cry. She asked me kindly: "What is the matter, Isaac?" I told her, "I wanted to see my mamma."

She tried to pacify me by saying: "Don't cry and fret about that, Isaac, you will see your mother again, Master will buy her and the rest of them sometime."

I asked: "Why didn't he buy them when he bought me?"

She replied: "My boy, never mind about that, your mother will be sold again soon and you will be together once more."

I asked: "Who bought her?"

Her reply was: "Never mind who bought her, you must not ask questions about such things, not a question, my word is law."

Soon thereafter Master and Peter returned; on entering the house Master asked: "Well, Margaret, how did you get along with the lad?"

THE JOHNSON CHILDREN.

She informed him that I had done nicely and that I was a good little worker.   His next inquiry was: "Have you taught him how to talk?"

"No," she replied, "but he'll learn without any trouble."

"That's the next thing he must learn," he said and then he called in a loud commanding tone: "Isaac, come here!"

"All right," I answered.

In an angry voice he said: "All right?   Is that the way you answer your Master?   When I tell you to 'come here' I want you to say, 'Yes, sir, Master.'   Now I'll try you once more; Isaac come here."

I was frightened and again said, "All right."

He was angry.   He took up the whip and said: "Isaac, you nigger you, if you don't talk to me as you ought to I shall use this black snake on you.   When I call you, you must say, 'yes, sir, Master,' and to your Mistress you must say, 'yes, Madam,' and don't you ever let me hear you say 'all right' to a white man, and when you meet a white man always take off your hat and say 'yes sir,' or 'no sir,' and stand to one side till he passes. Remember what I have told you or I shall try the black snake on your back.   Now go and help Peter do the chores."

I went, but you can imagine with what a heavy heart. Had it not been for the hope of again seeing my mother and brothers, I would gladly have lain down to die. Why should I be treated in this way; and still this was but the beginning of my new experiences.   I helped Peter about the barn, after which we returned to the house for supper.   We were allowed only two meals a day and mush and milk were not very lasting.   After supper, which was about 5:30 o'clock, Peter and I were sent to the corn crib to shell corn which was done by beating the ears with sticks very much the shape of hockey clubs. We were required to work at this till about ten o'clock at night during the winter, as long as the corn lasted.

As soon as spring came we were employed in cultivating the land, plowing, sowing, planting and hoeing. During this season of the year new hands were brought in every few days. One of these new hands was called "Jim." A few days later there were among those brought in a woman and her child, she was "Amelia," and her child was called "Lucy."

After the regular work was finished on the farm we were then set to clearing new land. Amelia was the cook and she had been there but a short time when she and the Mistress fell out. Amelia, to get even with the Mistress, put turpentine in the breakfast food, thinking it would poison the family; it didn't, however, but it made us all sick. The next day two men came and took Amelia away and left her child. What became of her we never knew, but her child was sent to a neighbor's. In a few days Master purchased another woman to take the place of Amelia, by the name of Anna, and harvesting the various crops commenced.

CHAPTER V.

HIRED OUT.

The harvesting was finally all done and the first day of January, 1853, had arrived. The first of January was the time when local sales and hiring took place. Myself, Jim and Peter were among those to be hired out and we were taken to Bardstown for this purpose. Our services for the year were sold at auction. Jim was sold for $150, Peter for $125, and I was sold for

$100.   The cook, Anna, was taken along and sold out-
right to the slave dealers, and that was the last we knew
of her.   Peter and Jim were hired by one Miller, a
farmer on the Columbia river, and I was hired to one
Yates, a store keeper in Hart county.   His store was
near the Mammoth cave, around which at that time was
a wilderness.   His family consisted of himself, his wife,
two sons, a woman slave and myself.   My work was to do
the chores about the house and run on errands to the store
which was about a mile distant.   I had a fairly easy
time here, my hardest work being to carry water from
the cave to the house, the distance being about a mile.
I had a yoke which laid across my shoulders, at each end
were hooks so I could carry two pails at once.   To get
the water I had to enter the cave and descend about
thirty feet.   I was always afraid when I entered the
cave because people told all manner of stories about it,
saying that there were all kinds of devils and animals
living in there who just delighted in catching colored
people and killing them.

     I managed, so far as I could, to go to the cave when
the sun was shining bright so that I could see my way
clearly to run if the devil appeared.   The two sons of the
Master were very mischievous, and when they learned
how afraid I was they would go each Sunday and build
a fire inside the cave and then send me for water.   When
I entered the cave and saw the fire I was sure it was
the devil, and would run screaming at the top of my
voice much to their amusement.   They would then go
back with me and enter the cave, by which time the fire
would be out, and they would then accuse me of lying
about seeing the devil.   This occurred so often that
Master became suspicious.   He asked why it was the
devils only appeared on Sundays.   This I could not

explain. He concluded to investigate for himself, and
the next Sunday went with me and caught the boys
building the fire, and that ended the stories of devils
being in the cave and I had no more trouble. I remained at this place till Christmas, when we were given
a week's holiday, and on the first of January, 1854, I
was sent to my Master's brother, his name was James
Madinglay. I remained with him two months. He
was the meanest kind of a slave holder. He had two
slaves, a girl and a boy. He drank very hard and sel-
dom left his room on account of his being too drunk to
do so. He would order the slaves to his room and whip
them unmercifully without any cause or provocation.
His son was equally as mean as he, he would watch the
slaves, and if he saw one idle, only for a moment, he
would inform his father and that meant, every time, a
severe whipping. We were to husk corn one morning
during the husking season, but it rained so very hard
that we did not start at once for the crib. For this delay
Master called us all in to be punished. I stood by and
saw him whip the other boy severely. I knew my turn
would come next, and I started on the run for home as
hard as I could run, not stopping till I reached there.
Mistress saw me and wished to know my reasons for my
appearance. I told her what had taken place and she
said: "All right, stay here till your Master comes
home."

I didn't know what Master would say or do, but when
he came I told him all about it. He listened quietly till
I was through, and then said: "It is all right this time,
Isaac, as I have rented my farm for four years and sold
you to my brother, John, who lives on the Beech Fork
river, about six miles from here; he is not at home now
but will be in a few days, so you can 'back' your things
and I will take you there in the morning."

I felt very well satisfied with the result and said: "I have nothing to 'back' as all I have is on my back and I can go any time."

The next day we went to his brother John's farm. There was no one there except the overseer and an old negro woman. The overseer's name was Steward, and he had been engaged to manage what was called "an improved stock farm." In a few days my new Master sent to the farm a fine looking slave girl, an octoroon, she was to take charge as stewardess. Master had won her at a game of poker in St. Louis. This girl he kept for his own use, and she was made Mistress of the stock farm. By stock it will be understood is meant negro slaves.

The stock soon began to arrive, there was a negro with a couple of brood mares, then came Jim and Peter, then two males, then three women, then about the first of **April John Madingly made his appearance with a** group of twenty, making thirty slaves all told. There were also brought onto the farm, farming utensils, mules, ten horses, thirty head of cattle, one hundred hogs and fifty sheep. He owned one thousand acres of land, but most of it was covered with brush or bushes. He raised the usual farm products and when these did not require attention we were set to work clearing the land. He had agents out in the country buying slaves and forwarding them to the farm, and soon there were one hundred and twenty slaves on the farm. After harvesting, the surplus negroes were sent to the Southern markets at Grand Gulf, Jackson and Vicksburg, at each of which places he had slave pens.

The time of the removal was kept secret from the slaves, and about ten o'clock the night before, twelve men were sent into the cabins and there handcuffed the males. In the morning these were brought out by twos and fastened to a chain about fifty feet long. The women and children not able to walk were packed into wagons and the line of march commenced, the chained men first, the women able to walk next, and the wagons brought up the rear. A beautiful sight for a country that boasts of its freedom! How the boasted Southern chivalry must have delighted in such sights, delighted in them so greatly they were ready to go to war to preserve the "sacred institution" of human slavery! I nave tasted its sacredness and felt that its Divinity is devlish. The line of march was to Nashville where they were placed aboard of boats and taken to the different slave pens.

The pens were divided into groups, women in one, men in another, girls and young boys by themselves. Here the buyers came and examined the stock, feeling of them as men do horses, looking into their mouths and eyes and asking questions as to sickness. Then the sales commenced and were held from November till about the first of March, during which time the agents were scouring the country, picking up new stock and forwarding the same to the market. After the first of March, if there were any unsold, they were taken back to the stock farm to work during the summer and shipped with the next lot ready for market.

The year 1857 was at hand. Fifteen slaves had been left on the farm to do the winter work. These were kept busy husking and shelling corn, taking it to the mill, then to the distillery and then made into liquor. That year of 1857 there were from five to six hundred barrels of liquor made and stored in the cellar. Master at this time was about sixty years of age and he married a girl about seventeen. He returned to the farm with his young wife, twelve slaves besides the stewardess, named Rosa, and trouble soon began.

Rosa was well fitted for her position and she had a general oversight of all the slaves. She was an octoroon and had the confidence of Master who trusted her to the utmost.

New slaves were brought in every few days and these were set to work during the summer, clearing land when there was no other work, their hours of labor being from 16 to 18 each day.

The slaves were divided into gangs, and over each gang was a Boss, who was also one of the slaves. At four o'clock each morning, the bell was rung and each Boss had to see that his gang was up and ready to commence the day's work. They marched by gangs to the tables set up under some trees in the yard, where breakfast was served for which one-half hour was allowed, after which each Boss marched his gang to the fields or to the kind of work laid out for them. The overseer rode on horse back from one gang to another seeing that all were kept busy. If he saw two or three idle, or talking to each other, if no satisfactory reason could be given, a whipping was sure to follow. At no time were three allowed to talk together unless the overseer was present. At twelve o'clock the gangs were marched to the tables for dinner, and one hour was allowed for dinner and rest, and then they were marched again to their work, where they remained as long as there was daylight to work by, and then they were marched once more to the tables for supper, after which they went to their cabins, each cabin being occupied by from ten to twelve persons, men and women were in separate cabins, except where they were married, and such had cabins by themselves. At ten o'clock the bell was rung when all must go to bed, or at half past ten, when the overseer made his rounds, if any were found up they were taken to the punishment room, and in the morning Master administered such punishment as he thought best. The punishment was a certain number of lashes from the whip for the first offence and more if the offence was repeated, with the addition of an iron weight tied to their backs for a number of days or weeks according to the Master's pleasure, these weights to be carried during the day while they were at work.

The year of which we are writing, about two hundred slaves were gathered on the stock farm, and in the fall most of them were marched off to the several slave markets in the same manner as before described, fastened to a long chain with the women who could walk following, and the women and children not able to walk in wagons. Of the two hundred, 170 were taken, leaving thirty to run the farm and do the winter work. This lot was taken to Bardstown, thence to Louisville, where they were put aboard of boats rigged with stalls similar to horse stalls into which the slaves were placed and chained until they reached Vicksburg or other places where markets were held.

On this trip Rosa accompanied the Master, and his wife was left on the farm to attend to matters there. His wife was a devout Catholic, and while Master was gone she used to gather the slaves remaining, each morning in her dining room and teach them prayers and some of the younger ones she taught to read. When the Master returned in the spring and learned what she had been doing he was very angry. He had always told his slaves that he was their Lord and Master, and now informed them his wife should not have told them of any other Lord. From Rosa we learned that he lectured his wife for her conduct about as follows: "If you teach them to pray and read they may think they are human beings and we will not be able to keep them as slaves; the more ignorant we keep them about such things the better slaves they are. The worst slaves we have are those who know the most, they are the ones we have to punish to keep them down. We have here from twenty to two hundred slaves each year, and if they should know as much as we do, where would we be? They would murder us in spite of the law. After this, my dear wife, you must never teach a negro the Lord's prayer, or any other prayer.

After the above there was no more gathering for prayers, and the little prayer books she had distributed among us and the little primers she had given were taken from us by Rosa, she saying: "The Master says you do not need them." Thus we soon lost what little we had learned, except, for some reason, the Lord's prayer, so simple and yet so full of meaning and comfort, was quite generally remembered. It has always seemed to me that there was some Divine help in this. That little prayer increased my wonder why we should be the slaves of the whites, and especially did I wonder in my own case when I thought of the fact that my mother was from the island of Madagascar and her people were never slaves. Why then should I be one?

After Master's lecture to his wife she had no more to do with us and the care of the slaves was turned over to Rosa, who was a slave herself, and the Sunday following, Master had us all seated on the ground in the yard and lectured us as follows:

"You must not think hard of me for telling you the truth about yourselves and the Whites. The great God above has made you for the benefit of the Whiteman, who is your law maker and law giver. Whenever you disobey his commands you must expect punishment. Your duty is in all cases to never raise your hand against a Whiteman and whenever you meet a Whiteman, no matter who or what he is, you must stop, take off your hat and stand to one side and say, 'Good day, Master,' or 'Good evening,' as the case may be. By doing this you do what is right on your side. You must understand you are just the same as the ox, horse, or mule, made for the use of the Whiteman and for no other purpose. You must do as the Whiteman tells you, if you do not he will punish you just the same as he would the mule when he breaks him. If you can't break the mule I tell you to kill him and that is the same with you. If you don't do what is right by me, why, my duty is to kill you just as I tell you to kill the mule if he doesn't do what is right. There is no more harm in me killing you than there is in you killing the mule, and I now say to you, if the mule doesn't do what is right—kill him! That is the law that you must go by."

CHAPTER VI.

BOB, THE CANADIAN.

Among the five slaves brought back to the stock farm unsold, was one named Bob who had come from Canada. He was an engineer and had hired on the steamer Louisville at Cincinnati, Ohio, for the round trip. When they reached New Orleans the cargo was sold, and just as the boat was ready to return, the sheriff came aboard and all negroes found who were not owned by a Whiteman were taken to the city jail, advertised for three months as runaway slaves, and if no owner claimed them they were sold to the highest bidder. This is the way Bob became a slave. At the sale of Bob, my master, John Madinglay, was the purchaser. He took him to

Grand Gulf and not being able to sell him there he brought him to the stock farm where he was placed in the hoe gang over which I was boss. My gang consisted of six boys and six girls besides Bob and myself. Bob was a shrewd as well as a powerful man. He was closely watched and not allowed to talk to any of the men, though he could at all times talk to and associate with Rosa and was encouraged to do so. The result was, Bob fell deeply in love with Rosa and talked with her freely. He told her all about his home and life in Canada and proposed that she go there with him. He pictured to her how pleasantly they could live in that land of freedom, where colored people were treated as human beings, and he laid before her all his plans to escape. She apparently consented to his proposals and the time was fixed when they were to start. The stock farm was on the banks of Beech Fork river, and whenever there was a heavy rain this river was swollen to a flood. When this should next occur was the time fixed upon for escape, and I was to go with them, though at first I did not know that Rosa was to go with us.

The flood soon came. I had charge of the skiff and watched eagerly till the water was at its height, when I informed Bob of the situation. I explained to him how we could get over the dams in safety. It was Saturday and I proposed to Bob that we start that night, and when evening came I urged Bob to start at once. But Bob said "No!" He was going to take Rosa with him. This was the first I knew of his intentions with reference to Rosa and I told him not to trust her, that she told everything she knew to Master. He refused to start that night, but said he would go next Monday morning as the Master was going away that day and would not return till night. I told him that would never do and tried to impress him with the fact that Rosa could not be trusted;

but he insisted that I leave the matter to him and everything would be all right. I was finally persuaded to
do as he said. Monday morning came and I got the
horse for Master who said he was going to town and told
me to go to the field to my work. On reaching the
field I informed Bob Master had gone and there was the
skiff. At this point of the river there was an elbow
around which the distance was ten miles, while across
the land it was only three miles. Bob told me to take
the boat around the elbow and he and Rosa would meet
me by going across the land. I started. The current
was strong and I made the distance in good time, reached
the other side but no Bob or Rosa was there. I waited
and waited for them for about three hours when I concluded to wait no longer. Bob had explained to me the
whole route to be taken to reach Canada and so I started
alone. I continued down stream till about seven o'clock
in the evening. I was halted during the day three different times by men on the shore who had guns and shot
at me. The first shot struck the boat but did not injure
it. Soon after I was shot at twice, but neither of them
came near me. This gave me courage and I thought:
"Fire away! you can't hit me!" Still I pulled harder
than ever and soon reached the railroad bridge and
passed under without being seen. About half a mile
inland I saw a light which I took for a negro cabin. I
was fearfully hungry, having had nothing to eat since
morning. I pulled my boat ashore and started for the
light. After I had gone two or three hundred yards the
light disappeared and I started back to the boat. As I
drew near I saw two men armed and they had two dogs
with them. I turned and ran for a swamp near by, the
men and dogs following. I managed to keep out of their
way for a couple of hours or more. The number of men

had increased to ten and I saw there was no chance for me to escape and the longer I tried to evade them the worse it would be for me. I knew the character of the dogs and what I might expect from them if they should reach me before the men were near, and I gave myself up. One of the men said he would take me to his house till morning and then return me to Master. I was taken to the depot near by, where there were about fifty men armed, all of whom had been hunting for me. Although I was only a poor negro boy, ignorant and without arms, these men were thoroughly armed with guns, knives and dogs as if they were in pursuit of a wild and ferocious animal. I was taken to the house, given some supper, which I was glad to get as I was as hungry as a bear, was given a place to lie down in a corner, the man and his wife were in another corner in the same room, so also were the dogs. He bolted the door, laid his revolver on a table near his bed in which he and his wife slept.

I took in the situation and made up my mind to have that revolver before morning. I laid down determined not to sleep. My day's work, however, had been a hard one, harder even than it would have been in the field on the old stock farm. I had scarcely laid down before I was fast asleep and knew nothing whatever till the man called me in the morning. My disappointment was great. I feared I had lost my last chance for freedom, still I had a little hope left and did not wholly despair. I was given some breakfast and told to split some wood while he hitched the horses. I watched him, sideways, till he entered the barn and as soon as he was out of sight I took to my heels and ran for the swamp. I must have had a quarter of a mile start before he set the dogs on my track. I heard their loud baying and

quickened my speed.   If there is anything that will
make one almost fly through the air, it is one of those
blood hounds on his track, with the knowledge that unless he outstrips them he is liable to be torn in pieces.
It is no wonder to me that deer and other animals chased
by dogs become so fleet.   I have never since heard of
such a chase for a deer, but I think of this race of my
own, and I must say it has created in me a sympathy for
the animal and I would gladly banish by law, if I could,
all such manner of hunting.   I reached the swamp
pretty well exhausted.   Here I hid, and, as luck would
have it, the dogs passed on beyond me, baying at every
jump. After they had passed I ran for the river and followed it till about four o'clock in the afternoon.   If I
heard an alarm on one side of the river I swam to the
other side and continued my race.   I watched for a skiff,
not finding one, I concluded to make a raft.   I had one
about completed and was covering it with brush, in which
I hoped to hide from sight of those ashore, when I heard
the sound of dogs near by.   I did not have time to push
off the raft, so I plunged into the water, swam a short
distance to a big stump near the shore.   The water in
this river was almost as black as ink, and an object
could not be seen below its surface.   I sank in the water,
leaving only my nose and mouth above.   Here I lay
for some time.   There were five men on the shore and
the dogs were hunting up and down the bank.   At last
one of the dogs got the scent and started for me with a
yelp.   The men gathered at once on the bank and, point-
ing their guns at me, ordered me to swim ashore.   I
saw there was no further use in my trying to escape and
I surrendered.

I was taken to the nearest depot and thence to my Master, who paid fifty dollars for my recovery. I was taken to the garret in his home, handcuffed for the night, and, to make sure I would not escape again, Peter was handcuffed to me. The next morning Peter was released, shackels were placed on my legs, and I remained in this shape till about 10 o'clock, when Master and his brother William, who was his slave agent, came to the garret, took off the shackels, handcuffed my hands behind my back and took me to the punishment room or shanty where I saw Bob lying on a few boards, his throat cut and he was slowly dying in great misery. From him I afterwards learned that about half an hour after I left the field, Master and three slave drivers came to the still house, sent for Bob to come there, which he did, not mistrusting what was before him. As soon as he arrived the four men all pounced upon him like four ravenous wolves upon a lamb. He fought all of them till he was overpowered. They then drove four stakes in the ground and he was tied to these with his back up and the four men took turns lashing him with a raw hide whip, the black snake I have refrred to, until his back appeared like a piece of beefsteak pounded . They then took hot coals from the furnace and poured them over his back, after which they took him to the punishment cabin, shackled his feet, chained him to the punishment block and in the night two of them went into the cabin and cut his throat, taking care not to cut the jugular, but cutting just enough so he would die gradually in torture.

Bob's condition was a lesson to the rest of us, and no means were allowed to escape making it an impressive one. He lived in this condition for five days and then his poor soul took its flight to the region where it is

hoped no slave holder will ever have the privilege of
exercising his power over human beings.

Talk to me about human slavery being a "Divine institution!"   As well tell me the devil is a merciful God.
The system not only degraded the slave, but it degraded
the master even more.   Any man of the South who is a
descendant of a slave holder who upheld the system of
American slavery, ought to blush with shame for his degraded origin.   I have in me the blood of one such,
on the side of my father, and to me, my poor black negro
mother shines as an angel in comparison to a devil, and,
if I could, I would willingly draw from my veins every
drop of that white blood that goes pulsing through
my body received by way of my father.   It is the
only stain I have received from the laws of nature,
of which I am ashamed, while on the other hand, I
am proud of my negro blood.   Poor Bob's skin was
black, but his soul was pure and in the great future
where, we are taught, we shall be ruled by a just God,
what will be Bob's condition in comparison with those
who tormented and murdered him?   But, the worst of
all is, that Rosa, whom Bob loved and trusted, was his
betrayer.   The white blood in her tainted her so that
she was equally as bad as her ancestors.   Perhaps, however, there was some excuse for her.   She was bright
and intelligent beyond most of her people, or even many
of the whites, and it may be that she had learned to love
her Master and was blinded, by reason of this, to all
humanity for another.   Had she carried out all that she
promised to Bob and started to leave with him and been
captured, she would have shared his fate.   Perhaps she
was not strong enough to fully recognize the enormity of
her relations with her Master and maybe she hoped
those relations would some day be the means of her own

freedom. As bad as it is we do not wholly condemn when men are cast upon the ocean where sure death is before them unless they have food and then draw cuts to see which one shall die to furnish food for the others. Perhaps she regarded her own condition much like the above and acted as she did to save herself.   I do not know.   I would like to shield her if I could, but I sometimes fear she was the treacherous being Bob believed and she appeared to be.

Bob was at last dead and then followed his funeral. A box was made into which he was placed, all the slaves were brought to view his remains, a grave was dug, the improvised coffin was loaded into a cart and we all followed him to his burial. After the remains were lowered into the grave Master preached what was called a funeral sermon. The substance of his words were: "This negro, Bob, was a bad man.   I paid my money for him and I was his master.   You all know that if he had done right as you have done, he would never have been where he is.   He cut his own throat and beat me out of my money.   You know that I must be obeyed and if you do not obey me I must whip you; but he was so mean that whipping was of no use to him and it would have been better for you and me if his throat had been cut long ago. There isn't one among you but knows I have done right, as he was a mean, mean negro.   You must understand there is no Lord or God who has anything to do with any of you, as I alone am your Master, your maker and your law giver, and when you do what I tell you to do you will get along all right."

After Bob's condition had been impressed upon me sufficiently, as they thought, and before Bob had died, at the time they took me to see him, I was again taken to the garret, from there I was taken to a ladder which stood between the house and the garden. My clothes were taken off and I was strapped to this ladder. Master's wife came forward and said: "Let him tell the whole truth about going away." I don't know, but I think she wished to implicate Rosa. Knowing that Bob was the same as dead and could not be hurt any further. I told them "I was going to Canada because there I would be a free man." Master then asked: "Who told you that Canada is a country in which you can be free?"

I said: "Bob told me."

He asked how many of the negroes knew about the runaway and I told him, "not one that I knew of."

He said: "Don't you know that you are lying to me? Doesn't Rosa know all about it?"

I told him, "No! if I thought she knew about it I would not have started, because I knew she would tell you."

He asked: "Are you sure none of the other negroes know anything about it?"

I answered, "I am sure, so far as I know."

The Mistress then said: "Isaac, I don't want to see you killed the same as Bob has been; if you will go in the garden and obey my orders I will see that your Master does not hurt you. I want you to never speak to a negro on the place, nor leave the garden without my permission, and when you come to meals come to my dining room and Rosa will serve you and at night you must go to the garret to sleep."

She then spoke to her husband, saying: "Let him go and I will look after him."

I was put in the garden which was surrounded by a high fence, the gate was locked and the key was given to Rosa so that I could not get out without her knowing it.

The above occurred before Bob had died. After I had been in the garden two days, Master and his wife went to visit a neighbor. After they had gone Rosa came to the garden and I asked her to allow me to go and see Bob. She had always been friendly with me and consented, saying, however: "You can go, but do not allow anyone to see you, if you do it will make trouble for me." I went. Bob could talk, but his voice was very weak. It was then he told me the particulars I have related about their treatment of him, and that he had been betrayed by Rosa. He also said: "Isaac, there is just one thing that I want to do before I die, and that is to punish Master. I am shackled and chained and can't get three feet from the bed. I want you to bring me a hatchet, ax, or something, and I will be satisfied."

I told him I could not do that as I was watched, but that I would get him the prong of a pitch fork. I went to the garden, got the prong, hid it under my shirt, picked some onions and asked Rosa if I could take the onions to Bob. She consented and I took them to him and left the pitchfork prong which he concealed about his bed and waited for a chance to get even with the Master. But Master was too cautious for him and did not go into the place till Bob had been dead some six hours.

CHAPTER VII.

THE YEARS 1859 AND 1860.

During the year 1859 Master had gathered on the stock farm one hundred and twenty negroes and all but ten were taken away to market. These were taken away in the same manner as others had been and all

were sold except two who were brought back to the farm
in the spring of 1860; and during the summer he
gathered about eighty more. After the crops were in
and harvested these eighty slaves were taken to market,
but in the meantime, Abraham Lincoln, God bless his
memory, had been elected President. There was no
market for the negroes and they were brought back to
the farm in the spring of 1861. The war had commenced by this time and slave property was at a dis-
count, and he bought no more.

It was then freely talked among the slaves that we
would soon all be free. Next, the Yankee soldiers began
to appear in the state and I concluded, "Now is the
time to make a break for liberty."

I heard there were troops within two miles and on
the following Sunday I started. But I soon found I
had made a mistake, as the troops proved to be Confederates from our own state. I was arrested and put
into the guard house. The guard house was a large tent
with a guard stationed in front. A severe storm came
that night and blew down the tent which caused quite a
confusion, during which I gave the guard the slip and
ran for home which I reached without my absence having
been discovered. I remained at home for a year, till
one day there was a Michigan regiment's train which
came within a mile of the farm.

I was at the mill that day and saw them. I made a
bargain with one of the men to go and cook for his captain. That night after my work was done I started and
about one o'clock I overtook the train. The guard
halted me: I said I was a friend and he told me:
"Advance friend and give the countersign." I advanced
but I had no countersign when he wished to know what
I was doing there that time of night? I told him I

had hired with one of the men to come and cook for his captain. He told me if that was so it was all right and took me to the wagons where we found the man who had hired me. I turned in with him for the rest of the night and in the morning he gave me a breakfast and a new suit of soldier clothes. I drove a team to Lebanon where I met Captain Smith of the Eighth Michigan, captain of Company A, and hired out to him for seven dollars per month, the first money I had ever had a chance to earn and call my own. I was then eighteen years of age. We lay in camp a few weeks and then went to Green river. While at this place I had a letter written to Rosa telling her of my good fortune, but the Master got the letter. He, with a negro driver soon started for the camp. I saw them while I was by a brook washing some clothes for my captain. I mistrusted they were after me and hid near the road where I remained till I saw them go away, when I took the clothes to my tent.

The captain came in and asked: "Isaac, what are you looking so down-hearted for?"

I said: "Nothing in particular."

He then said: "Oh, yes, Isaac, there is something wrong."

He answered: "I suppose you saw your Master?"

I said: "I did, but he didn't see me."

"Well," said he, "your Master has been here after you, he went to the colonel and asked for you. The colonel was indignant and told him he hadn't come here to make himself a blood hound to hunt runaway negroes and then said he would give him just fifteen minutes to get outside of his lines, and your Master started without asking any more questions."

The captain then called me into his tent, gave me a revolver and twenty rounds of cartridges saying: "Take these and protect yourself, that is all we have to protect ourselves and if any man comes to demand your liberty, shoot him as you would a dog, if you don't, you ought to be a slave.

Oh what a feeling of manhood came to me with those words. I felt myself a man, every inch of me. It was my second taste of freedom, the hiring for wages being the first. I took the revolver and cartridges and made up my mind to follow directions if I should be molested and that I would deserve my freedom. I remained with Captain Smith till his term had expired. He and many of his regiment re-enlisted, they were given a furlough and I accompanied him home to Detroit.

CHAPTER VIII.

FULL MANHOOD AT LAST.

After we got to Detroit, I could look across and see the happy land of Canada, to me a Canaan, of which I had heard so much, for which I had yearned, and of which I had dreamed sleeping and awake. I never step my feet upon Canadian soil, even to this day, without a feeling of love and respect for its people, and "God bless you!" instinctively comes to my thoughts. I told the captain I thought I should go to Canada where I was sure to be free from all masters. He wished me to stay and return with him to the army. I told him, "No! I shall never return unless I can go as a soldier."

He then informed me they were getting up a colored regiment in that city at that time, and if I desired to fight for myself and my race I had better enlist with that regiment, and I did so in short order.

I accordingly enlisted in Company A, 102 United States Colored troops, and I remained with them till the war was over. After the close of the war I had a strong desire to return to the old Kentucky home to see my old Master and to learn what I could of my own people. I think I also had a desire to see Master in the broken condition I imagined the war must have left him. I started and reached the old stock farm at last where I had seen so much misery. I went to the house and found master was in bed, paralyzed. He had not been out of his bed for six months. I said to myself: "The Lord has answered my prayer and allowed me to live to see him punished who so cruelly tortured and murdered my friend Bob."

Master was apparently glad to see me. He said I was the first to leave him and the first to return. With the old time Southern hospitality he sent to the cellar for something to drink and I was made welcome to the best in the house. I could not help but notice the change. There were two ex-Confederates in the room who did not look upon me very kindly, if I read them aright. Master offered me good wages if I would only return and remain while he lived. I think, perhaps, I may have given him, from prudential motives, some hopes that I would do so. But I knew him too well to think of it seriously. I found Rosa, who had married one of the Draper colored people across the river. The Drapers were Catholics and were always good to their slaves, never selling one to a slave trader. She was a happy woman in her new relations and her husband was industrious and prosperous. I could not learn anything of my own people, but I saw my father's brothers, who told me some of the things herein related. They had never heard from my father after he caused us to be sold.

Master never left his bed. With all my negro blood and all that I have passed through, I would rather be in my black skin than in his or my father's.   Think of being obliged to associate with men of their stamp, say nothing about being their slaves. The mere thought is repulsive.   A man who could sell his own children or who would uphold a system that enabled him to do so—the thought is a horror.   My people, for I call only the colored people mine, suffered for centuries, and the only wonder to me is that so many have survived, that they are as intelligent as they are, and as forgiving as they have shown themselves to be.

A race with such natural characteristics comes nearer to the teachings of the great Master than any people of whom I have learned.   The manner in which they have used their freedom and treated their former masters appears to me they must have indelibly stamped in their natures the Lord's teachings, wherein He says: "But I say unto you, love your enemies, bless them that curse you, do good to them that hate you and pray for them which despitefully use you and persecute you, that you may be the children of your Father who is in heaven."

To be worthy to be counted one who lives up to the above is my desire, notwithstanding all I have experienced.

In order that my relatives may know where to find me, in case this little pamphlet should fall into their hands, I give my Post Office address:

ISAAC JOHNSON,

21 Main Street, Ogdensburg,

St. Lawrence Co., N. Y.